Blue Tongue

Poems and drawings
By
Jasper Morley

'Hazelwood'

Summer Skies

There is a land of summer skies
A swarming with a billion flies
If you ignore them
They don't bother you
After a while

Hazelwood Park's swimming pool
After a day at Burntside school
No bombing is the broken rule
In and out and staying cool

Lying on poolside concrete
Naples yellow and the texture of coarse sandpaper
The water on their fronts
Cools the blue pool's yellow frame just quickly enough
For it not
To be too too hot

For the briefest of moments the boys enjoyed being
warmed by the solid heat
The water trapped between sapling trunks and the hot block
Soon warms to the tepid temperature of sweat
And it is time for chlorine clean cooling

That chemical which gives some sun bleached blonde hair
Statue of liberty green highlights
The crude damp headless impressions
Of their bodies soon shrink

And disappear

Strawberry Redskins and spearmint White Knights
wrappers
There is a buzz of flies circling, swarming and entering
The open mouths of the metal penguin shaped bins
With their rancid sweet breath

Dressed in seconds with a series of haphazard twitches
They ratchet through the exit turnstiles
And trek across the park

Silent blue tongue eaten away by ants
Whose armies form a black line
Quivering with movement from nest to lizard lunch and
back again
They had eaten an entrance through the eyes

After a brief inspection of the lizard shell
They stare at a rainbow hovering over a huge sprinkler
Ticking rhythmically like a giant clock with arching watery
hands

They set themselves the task of hitting every tree
Along an avenue of massive gums
With a handful of stones
The trees high branches are dotted
With the bright colours of gas bagging parrots

The trees are unflinching as both boys' stones hit
their mark
As they have been for decades of boys stones
They have outlived many of the throwers whose
marks they bare
Two stones simultaneously hit the last tree in the
row
One stone carries complete satisfaction
And the other the slightest hint of regret

Body

Sacred heart
Obsession

Treasure chest
Repression

Piggy back
Aggression

A little Bird Told Me

Lake Albert

It takes the minds of children to find amusement
And not to be baked with boredom
On such a long straight road
On such a long hot day
In the crowded sweaty backs, backseat of the family wagon

'She was just thirty one,
And she weighed three hundred ton,
And the way she looked was way beyond repair.
I'd rather dance with my brother, yuck
When I saw her standing there'
The boys rewrote the Beatles
Especially for their Mum
She was carrying their new sister
In her large and rounded tum

They passed petrol mile
A row of petrol stations that stretched for a mile
Through Murray Bridge
A town on the Murray with a bridge they crossed
And around Talem Bend
The bend they were all driven around

To Lake Albert
A lake of sweat on their father's shirt
A muddy fresh water lake that had their father's name
Though he was known as John
That's where their Chrysler Valiant journey ends

At a grand mansion built on the Lakes distant shore
On the edge of the middle of nowhere
Standing alone with thick walls of stone
 An encircling veranda and a tin roof
Like the wide brim of a corrugated iron hat

Built for a prince that never came
A holiday farm became it's hoped for trade
City livestock
Of varied grade

The impressive front parlour
Was the coolest room in the house
For a friendly game of cards
Make sure you pick out the three cornered Jacks
Sticking in your flip flops
There was a majestic black marble unlit fire surround
A dishevelled shiny shell of an antique clock

Silent time at centre of the mantelpiece
High ceilings and low stake poker
We played five kid card happy families
Without a full deck
Wars and depression had stripped the house
And picked the grounds clean
Of most of its original unvisited majesty

Some of the stripped jetties rotting stumps
Popped their dark decaying heads out of the lake

There were just enough stumps showing to make out a line
The others were a hidden hazard beneath the cloudy water
Waters with no tide but plenty of yabbies
Wandering in to one pot then another

Bowed legged farmer Chas
Went about the business
Of putting meat on the table

Sitting picking thorns from their flip flops
They sat outside listening to the shouting within
Cooked cottage holiday walls
'What are they shouting about?' the youngest asked
'Nothing really, it's the roaring forties' the oldest replied

She packed a bag a headed back for Adelaide and home
One hundred and seventeen and a half miles away
She headed off at sunset on foot
After a solid day of heated words
She had had enough and started to walk
They had had enough but were stuck in the thorny dust of
dusk
They trailed her in the Valiant at walking pace
Stopping when she stopped and went when she went
It started with a tickle and a trickle of a giggle
And ended with a flood of laughter

She fell at the first fence
A weighty iron gate
There was silence

Then she joined in as the laughter erupted again

The anger had been blown out of the water by their humour
A sixth sense that had ended the drama
Tears laughter and a bottle of warm fizz
Spearmint Knights and a sup of hot tea

Apart from a thin strip of beach
And the odd three corner jack free patch of grass
The surrounding landscape was as alluring as a dead
pelican or a bright coloured grub

And inspite of it being a family holiday there were
moments
That made it worth that long journey to a ruin by a distant
cloudy lake
Collecting yabby pots before the heat of the day
Keeping cool in pine scented evening breeze
And watching cards spinning in the air
Waiting for a winning hand to land gently on a lucky
shoulder

'Famiglia'

Arrow Head

Bottle neck
Arrow head
Passed out pissed
On a dried up river bed

Drained
From a leaky mouth's roof
Brained
In sick stained truth
Snake bitten bombardier
White lightning has struck you down
You were bitten and bombed
Sucking sour sobs
You have been drunk dry by those who
kept you alive
To feed on your sorrow

'Short Passage 1'

Hapless

Hapless and happy
Mapless and chatty
A feral cat
Sometimes a bit ratty

The mungrel child
Of toffs and strays
From a colonial, baronial
Dusty maze

He is now
A crazy cat
Hissy hippie spit
That a Beatnik spat

With lumps and bumps
Scars and patches
In dumps with chumps
With a shirt that scratches

The cat catcher caught him
With the use of medication

It made him a lap cat
Earmarked for castration

They liked to stroke him
Bu they hit a wound
Then the pain started
And the madness ballooned

His shackles raised,
In hissy fitting
Claws out, eyes clenched
Crying and spitting

They were shocked at his carry on
And so pretty soon
Wanted him gone
That volatile loon

They threw him out
And shut the door
They couldn't cope
With him anymore

If they didn't want him
Hanging around
They should stop feeding and needing him
When they want company

 Don't worry about him
He can fend for himself
He's stopped taking the pills
They were bad for his health

Let them stroke
Their smelly black dogs
All of his friends are
Are the coolest of mogs

I don't have pets
I don't see vets
And yes I do
Have regrets

But I've decided
I'm breaking free
I am getting out
There's things to see

They can keep their scraps
And locking flaps
Their whinging and whining
And bony laps

I am taking off
As the birds suggested
I am not waiting round
To get molested

I'm forced by nature
Out of the way
They're shut in
I'm off to play

'Second Hand'

Magpies

Swing your satchels
Over your head
Or frisky magpies
Will peck your head
You're too old
To wet your bed
You'll go crazy
If you chew lead
Eating lots of carrots
Makes your hair go red
So don't let the magpies
Peck your head
Until the fat policeman
Shoots them dead

One for sorrow
Two for joy
The teacher takes a girl
And the farmer takes a boy

'First Hand'

Mum and Dad

Mum and Dad
Dumb and mad
Just a minute son
Was it so bad?

Now look what you made me do
So said Mum
It's thanks to you
Did I say that?
Or was it you?

Mum and Dad
Dumb and mad
Yes I'm angry
Yes I'm sad
For ending up
So dumb and mad

I have a scar on my shin
On which the skin is very thin

It starts to bleed
Every now and then

You nursed me
You blessed me
You cursed me
You dressed me

I could think myself numb
About my Dad and my Mum
But I am Dumb and I am Mad
And ended up like
Mum and Dad

'Drawn Out Conversation'

Hillcrest

Bright hard hot, fine loose gravel and dust
A dirt track as loose and hard
as childhood memories
I was big enough to tip my head
sideways out of the car window
Squinted eyes and face,
blasted with hot air in the full glare of the day
I could only act like a dog for so long
I pulled my head in and stuck out my arm instead
I allowed my guided flattened hand
to fly in the air flow
The road was new world wide
and roman straight leading to the crest of a hill

We were out of town, out of sight and out of 'Minties'
We had passed the abattoir with its renowned stench
I was glad to tell my schoolmates
'I had smelled the worst smell I had ever smelled'
I checked it many times
to be sure of its putrid greasy rankness

We passed Yatla where its inmates sweated it out and
I wondered what sort of a mate an inmate was
We passed a scrapyard a car-yard cement works and a
dump
I looked on in fascination and searched for the black stump

We were headed to, out there somewhere

What was it that the populous found
more offensive than the smell and function of the abattoir?
And what was it they felt more threatening
than the penned in mates of Yatla

Over the hill grand gates came in to view
The grandest gates I had ever seen
Was this a hidden wonderland?
Once through the gates
it was a relief to glide smoothly and
quietly along the bitumen drive
after miles of rattling, grinding dirt road
The long drive wound its way to the grandness
suggested by the nudge in the ribs that the gates had given
An impressive colonial façade stood
at the centre of well watered lawns and parkland

But there were wire fences
municipal signs and crude new modern extensions
Something did not fit
Way out there beyond the scrapyard and dump
A hospital, a different hospital
And behind the walls, and heavily gated home
Way out there, were outsiders

'Circulation'

Underpass

He's from the back row of the underclass
He graduated with an underpass
He was taught very little
And he learnt even less
Is it any wonder
His life is in a mess?

He didn't start out in the underclass
He only ended up there
After living under glass
He has many opinions
But few beliefs
He hasn't found the answers
On temple's stone reliefs

The fear of being a victim
Of others remote control

Means he's not surrendered,
His heart, his mind or soul

Not to one god, or ideology,
One theory or mythology
To bio-eco-psycho-micro-
Macro-sociology

He's trying to keep his heart from seeking
Answers not meant for keeping
In trying to end this paned impasse
He's in the back row of the underclass

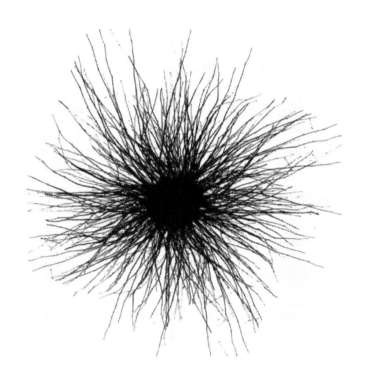

'Self-Seed'

Sticky Bun

Stick the world in a bun
Throw it at the sun

Planes hanging from a thread
Thunderbird eyebrows
Unmade bed

Animals in an envelope
Marbles in my slipper
Hazy sunshine
Sherbet dipper

Still There

I followed a trail of Monarch
butterflies
Dead and dying in their thousands
Flickering black and gold
On grey gravel
By the side of the road
Around Devil's elbow
That nudges weary drivers
Approaching Adelaide

I got to the top of Mt Lofty
And barely paused
Then down I went
Down Waterfall Gully
And up the other side

I sat on Elephant rock
And rode on the back of snaking
daydreams
Motionless in the sun like a blue
tongued lizard
Basking in childhood freedom

Still there in the hot still air
Are thoughts that slipped my mind
Unknowable recollections
Part of me is safe

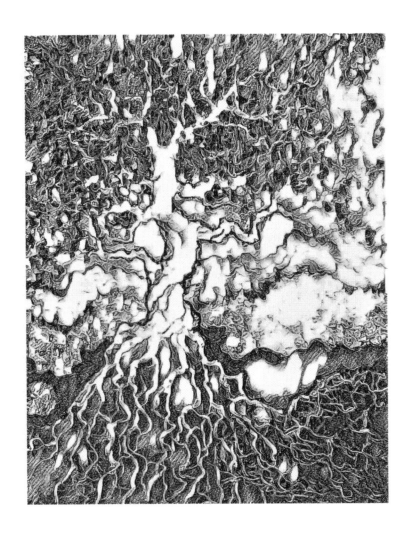

'Arboreal'

Estuary

On the tide
Of narrow eyed
Silted tears
A life flows by

Carried to a vast ocean
Of fluid souls
Pulled by the moon
That makes the earth draw breath

A vessel is emptied
Into the stream

Just below the surface
A milky cloud of ash
Unfolds into invisibility
And drifts away

Watching from the rocks
Three figures crouch

Waiting for the vibrations
Of the bell's fading note
To thin into silence

They stand together
They turn away
From a bridge
They look back one last time
Held between two moments
Two shores
Two states
Numb with cold uncertainty
They embrace for warmth
And peaceful hearts

'Home Grown'

Know

I know
I know you know
That's a know know

Begonia

Rich red Begonia petals drop, like thicker than water blood
onto a tangled yellow field of, sour sobs
And one lilac lonely Salvation Jane

The saturated, purple bruised, clouded sky, cries heavens
tears
Perhaps they were yours
You left so many un-cried on earth

The clouds lighten and roll away
The sky sings blue again
Until the next, Dr Pat's pipe tobacco, soggy handkerchief
cloud rolls in
And I will cry your un-cried tears for another year

'Parkway'

Oedipus

Oedipus
Ate a pussy
But it was his Mum's

Wasn't happy
With his Pappy
Shot him in his plums

'Headland'

Beneath

Maybe my mind has been poisoned
By the mercury in my teeth
Or maybe I was born this way
And formed by sun and grief
Whether damaged or flawed
What can't be ignored
Is the pain that lies beneath

Crowded Sleep

I woke from a crowded sleep
Of swollen eyes that could not
weep

I must find the reason why
Sleep again and let them cry

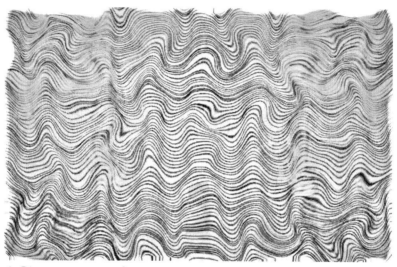

'Contours'

Sanctuary

On hot rocks
Behind the wall of an empty
overgrown plot
Under a bridge
Over land without skin
Between a curtain and a wall
Along the streets of a foreign town
In a vast unpeopled landscape

Sanctuary

Siblings

Quibbling siblings
Grappling saplings

Sou

r Sobs

There is no taste like a sour sob
 With its bright and yellow flower

And if you chance to bite its stalk
You'll find its sap is sour

Printed in Great Britain
by Amazon